50 The Art of French Cooking Recipes

By: Kelly Johnson

Table of Contents

- Classic Coq au Vin
- Beef Bourguignon
- Ratatouille Provençale
- Quiche Lorraine
- Croque Monsieur
- Duck Confit
- French Onion Soup
- Poulet Rôti (Roast Chicken)
- Escargots de Bourgogne
- Tarte Tatin
- Soupe au Pistou
- Bouillabaisse
- Salade Niçoise
- Gratin Dauphinois
- Cassoulet
- Chateaubriand with Béarnaise Sauce
- Potatoes Dauphine
- Pâté en Croûte
- Filet Mignon au Poivre
- Chicken Fricassée
- Sole Meunière
- Moules Marinières
- Foie Gras au Torchon
- Gâteau de Crêpes
- Tarte au Citron Meringuée
- Soufflé au Fromage
- Clafoutis aux Cerises
- Salade de Chèvre Chaud
- Bouchees à la Reine
- Croustillants de Brie
- Salade Landaise
- Poulet Basquaise
- Sauté de Veau à la Normande
- Pâtisserie Chouquettes
- Pissaladière

- Tartelette aux Framboises
- Côtelettes d'Agneau aux Herbes
- Crêpes Suzette
- Fennel and Orange Salad
- Blanquette de Veau
- Grilled Lobster with Herb Butter
- Chilled Vichyssoise
- Veal and Mushroom Ragout
- Confit de Canard
- Sablé Bretons
- Fricassée de Poulet
- Galette des Rois
- Poulet en Papillote
- French Macarons
- Pâté de Campagne

Classic Coq au Vin

Ingredients:

- 4 chicken thighs, bone-in, skin-on
- 2 tbsp olive oil
- 1 large onion, sliced
- 2 carrots, sliced
- 2 cloves garlic, minced
- 1 ½ cups red wine (preferably Burgundy)
- 1 cup chicken broth
- 1 tbsp tomato paste
- 1 bay leaf
- 2 thyme sprigs
- 10 small pearl onions, peeled
- 8 oz button mushrooms, halved
- Salt and pepper to taste
- Fresh parsley for garnish

Instructions:

1. Heat olive oil in a large Dutch oven over medium heat. Season the chicken thighs with salt and pepper, then brown them on both sides, about 6-8 minutes. Remove and set aside.
2. In the same pot, add the sliced onion, carrots, and garlic. Sauté for 5 minutes, until softened.
3. Stir in the tomato paste and cook for 1 minute. Pour in the wine and chicken broth, scraping the bottom of the pot to release any browned bits.
4. Add the bay leaf, thyme, and chicken back into the pot. Bring to a simmer, cover, and cook for 45 minutes, until the chicken is tender.
5. In a separate pan, sauté the pearl onions and mushrooms in a bit of oil until golden. Add them to the pot during the last 10 minutes of cooking.
6. Remove the chicken and vegetables, then reduce the sauce over medium heat until thickened, about 10 minutes. Return the chicken to the pot to warm through.
7. Garnish with fresh parsley and serve.

Beef Bourguignon

Ingredients:

- 2 lbs beef chuck, cut into 2-inch cubes
- 3 tbsp olive oil
- 1 large onion, chopped
- 2 carrots, sliced
- 3 cloves garlic, minced
- 2 cups red wine (preferably Burgundy)
- 1 cup beef broth
- 2 tbsp tomato paste
- 1 tbsp flour
- 2 bay leaves
- 3 thyme sprigs
- 10 oz pearl onions, peeled
- 8 oz button mushrooms, sliced
- Salt and pepper to taste
- Fresh parsley for garnish

Instructions:

1. Preheat oven to 325°F (165°C). Heat olive oil in a large Dutch oven over medium-high heat. Season the beef with salt and pepper and brown on all sides, about 8-10 minutes. Remove the beef and set aside.
2. In the same pot, add the onion, carrots, and garlic. Sauté for 5 minutes until softened.
3. Stir in the tomato paste and flour, cooking for 1 minute. Add the wine, beef broth, bay leaves, and thyme. Bring to a simmer, scraping the bottom of the pot.
4. Return the beef to the pot and cover. Transfer to the oven and cook for 2-2.5 hours, until the beef is tender.
5. In a separate pan, sauté the pearl onions and mushrooms until browned. Add them to the pot during the last 30 minutes of cooking.
6. Once done, remove the bay leaves and thyme. Garnish with fresh parsley and serve.

Ratatouille Provençale

Ingredients:

- 1 eggplant, diced
- 2 zucchinis, diced
- 1 red bell pepper, chopped
- 1 yellow bell pepper, chopped
- 1 onion, chopped
- 4 tomatoes, diced
- 3 cloves garlic, minced
- 1/4 cup olive oil
- 1 tsp dried thyme
- 1 tsp dried oregano
- Salt and pepper to taste
- Fresh basil for garnish

Instructions:

1. Heat olive oil in a large skillet over medium heat. Add the onion and garlic, sautéing for 3-4 minutes until softened.
2. Add the eggplant, bell peppers, and zucchini. Cook for about 10 minutes, stirring occasionally, until softened.
3. Stir in the tomatoes, thyme, oregano, salt, and pepper. Reduce heat and simmer for 15-20 minutes, until the vegetables are tender and the flavors have melded.
4. Garnish with fresh basil and serve hot.

Quiche Lorraine

Ingredients:

- 1 pre-baked pie crust (store-bought or homemade)
- 6 slices bacon, cooked and crumbled
- 1 cup Gruyère cheese, grated
- 1/2 cup heavy cream
- 1/2 cup milk
- 4 large eggs
- Salt and pepper to taste
- 1/4 tsp nutmeg (optional)

Instructions:

1. Preheat the oven to 375°F (190°C). Place the pre-baked pie crust on a baking sheet.
2. Evenly distribute the crumbled bacon and grated cheese into the pie crust.
3. In a bowl, whisk together the eggs, cream, milk, salt, pepper, and nutmeg. Pour the egg mixture into the pie crust.
4. Bake for 30-35 minutes, until the quiche is set and lightly golden on top.
5. Let cool slightly before slicing and serving.

Croque Monsieur

Ingredients:

- 8 slices white bread
- 4 slices ham
- 4 slices Gruyère or Swiss cheese
- 1 cup béchamel sauce (butter, flour, milk, nutmeg, salt, and pepper)
- 1 tbsp Dijon mustard
- Butter for toasting

Instructions:

1. Preheat the oven to 400°F (200°C).
2. Spread a thin layer of mustard on 4 slices of bread. Top with a slice of cheese, then a slice of ham, followed by another slice of cheese.
3. Top with the remaining bread slices.
4. Spread a thin layer of béchamel sauce over the top of each sandwich.
5. Butter the outside of each sandwich and toast in a pan over medium heat until golden on both sides.
6. Transfer to a baking sheet and bake for 10 minutes, until the cheese is melted and bubbly.
7. Serve hot.

Duck Confit

Ingredients:

- 4 duck legs, skin-on
- 4 cups duck fat (or enough to cover the legs)
- 4 cloves garlic, smashed
- 4 sprigs thyme
- 2 bay leaves
- Salt and pepper to taste

Instructions:

1. Preheat the oven to 300°F (150°C).
2. Season the duck legs with salt and pepper. Place them in a baking dish or Dutch oven, covering with duck fat.
3. Add the garlic, thyme, and bay leaves. Cover and bake for 2-3 hours, until the duck is tender.
4. To crisp the skin, heat a skillet over medium-high heat. Remove the duck legs from the fat and place them skin-side down in the pan. Sear for 3-4 minutes until crispy.
5. Serve with roasted potatoes or greens.

French Onion Soup

Ingredients:

- 4 large onions, thinly sliced
- 2 tbsp butter
- 1 tbsp olive oil
- 2 cloves garlic, minced
- 4 cups beef broth
- 1 cup dry white wine
- 1 tbsp fresh thyme or 1 tsp dried thyme
- 1 baguette, sliced
- 2 cups Gruyère cheese, grated
- Salt and pepper to taste

Instructions:

1. In a large pot, melt the butter with the olive oil over medium heat. Add the onions and cook, stirring frequently, for 40-50 minutes, until caramelized and golden.
2. Add the garlic and cook for another 2 minutes. Pour in the wine, scraping the bottom of the pot to deglaze.
3. Add the beef broth, thyme, salt, and pepper. Simmer for 20 minutes.
4. Ladle the soup into bowls. Top with baguette slices and grated cheese.
5. Place the bowls under the broiler for 3-5 minutes, until the cheese is bubbly and golden.
6. Serve hot.

Poulet Rôti (Roast Chicken)

Ingredients:

- 1 whole chicken (about 4-5 lbs)
- 2 tbsp olive oil
- 1 lemon, halved
- 1 bunch fresh thyme
- 4 garlic cloves, smashed
- Salt and pepper to taste

Instructions:

1. Preheat the oven to 425°F (220°C). Place the chicken in a roasting pan.
2. Rub the chicken with olive oil, then season generously with salt and pepper.
3. Stuff the cavity with the lemon halves, thyme, and garlic cloves.
4. Roast for 1 to 1.5 hours, until the chicken reaches an internal temperature of 165°F (75°C) and the skin is golden and crispy.
5. Let rest for 10 minutes before carving and serving.

Escargots de Bourgogne (Snails in Garlic Butter)

Ingredients:

- 24 escargots (snails), cleaned and shelled
- 4 tbsp unsalted butter, softened
- 3 cloves garlic, minced
- 1 shallot, finely chopped
- 2 tbsp fresh parsley, chopped
- 1 tbsp fresh thyme, chopped
- 1 tbsp white wine
- Salt and pepper to taste
- 12 escargot shells (or small ramekins)

Instructions:

1. Preheat the oven to 375°F (190°C).
2. In a bowl, mix together the softened butter, garlic, shallot, parsley, thyme, white wine, salt, and pepper.
3. Place one escargot in each shell or ramekin. Fill each shell with the garlic butter mixture.
4. Arrange the shells in a baking dish. If using ramekins, place them directly on a baking sheet.
5. Bake for 15-20 minutes, or until the butter is bubbling and the escargots are heated through.
6. Serve with crusty baguette slices to dip into the garlic butter.

Tarte Tatin

Ingredients:

- 6 medium apples (preferably Granny Smith or Braeburn), peeled, cored, and halved
- 1 cup granulated sugar
- 1/4 cup unsalted butter
- 1 tsp vanilla extract
- 1/2 tsp ground cinnamon (optional)
- 1 sheet puff pastry
- 1 tbsp lemon juice

Instructions:

1. Preheat the oven to 375°F (190°C).
2. In a 9-inch oven-safe skillet, melt the butter over medium heat. Add the sugar and cook, stirring occasionally, until it forms a golden caramel, about 5-7 minutes.
3. Add the apples to the caramel, arranging them in a circular pattern. Sprinkle with vanilla extract, cinnamon, and lemon juice.
4. Cook the apples for 15 minutes, occasionally spooning the caramel over them.
5. Roll out the puff pastry and place it over the apples, tucking the edges inside the skillet.
6. Transfer the skillet to the oven and bake for 25-30 minutes, until the pastry is golden and puffed.
7. Allow the tart to cool for 5 minutes, then carefully invert it onto a plate and serve warm.

Soupe au Pistou (Provençal Vegetable Soup with Basil Pesto)

Ingredients:

- 1 tbsp olive oil
- 1 onion, chopped
- 2 carrots, peeled and chopped
- 2 zucchini, chopped
- 2 cloves garlic, minced
- 4 cups vegetable broth
- 1 can (15 oz) cannellini beans, drained and rinsed
- 1 cup green beans, cut into 1-inch pieces
- 1 cup elbow pasta or other small pasta
- Salt and pepper to taste

For the Pistou:

- 2 cups fresh basil leaves
- 2 cloves garlic
- 1/4 cup olive oil
- 1/4 cup grated Parmesan cheese
- Salt to taste

Instructions:

1. In a large pot, heat olive oil over medium heat. Add the onion, carrots, zucchini, and garlic, and cook for 5 minutes, until softened.
2. Add the vegetable broth, cannellini beans, and green beans. Bring to a simmer and cook for 10-15 minutes.
3. Stir in the pasta and cook according to the package instructions, about 8-10 minutes.
4. While the soup simmers, make the pistou: blend the basil, garlic, olive oil, Parmesan, and a pinch of salt in a food processor until smooth.
5. Once the soup is ready, stir in 2-3 tablespoons of pistou and adjust seasoning with salt and pepper.
6. Serve hot, with extra pistou and grated cheese on the side.

Bouillabaisse (Provençal Fish Stew)

Ingredients:

- 2 tbsp olive oil
- 1 onion, chopped
- 2 leeks, cleaned and chopped
- 2 celery stalks, chopped
- 4 cloves garlic, minced
- 4 medium tomatoes, chopped
- 4 cups fish stock
- 1 cup dry white wine
- 1/2 tsp saffron threads
- 1 bay leaf
- 1 tsp fennel seeds
- 1 lb mixed fish (such as cod, snapper, and/or sole), cut into chunks
- 1/2 lb shellfish (mussels, clams, shrimp)
- Salt and pepper to taste

For the Rouille:

- 1 egg yolk
- 2 cloves garlic
- 1/2 tsp saffron threads
- 1/2 cup olive oil
- 1 tbsp lemon juice
- Salt and pepper to taste

Instructions:

1. In a large pot, heat olive oil over medium heat. Add the onion, leeks, celery, and garlic, cooking for 5-7 minutes until softened.
2. Add the tomatoes, fish stock, white wine, saffron, bay leaf, and fennel seeds. Bring to a simmer and cook for 20 minutes.
3. Add the fish and shellfish to the pot and simmer for 5-10 minutes, until the fish is cooked through and the shellfish has opened.
4. To make the rouille, blend the egg yolk, garlic, saffron, olive oil, lemon juice, salt, and pepper in a food processor until smooth.
5. Serve the bouillabaisse hot with the rouille spread on toasted baguette slices.

Salade Niçoise

Ingredients:

- 2 cups mixed greens (arugula, lettuce, etc.)
- 2 medium tomatoes, sliced
- 1/2 red onion, thinly sliced
- 1 cucumber, sliced
- 4 hard-boiled eggs, quartered
- 1 can (6 oz) tuna in olive oil, drained and flaked
- 12 black olives (preferably Niçoise or Kalamata)
- 1/4 cup olive oil
- 2 tbsp red wine vinegar
- 1 tbsp Dijon mustard
- Salt and pepper to taste

Instructions:

1. Arrange the mixed greens on a large platter or individual plates.
2. Top with tomatoes, onion, cucumber, hard-boiled eggs, tuna, and olives.
3. In a small bowl, whisk together the olive oil, vinegar, mustard, salt, and pepper.
4. Drizzle the dressing over the salad and serve immediately.

Gratin Dauphinois (Potato Gratin)

Ingredients:

- 2 lbs potatoes, peeled and thinly sliced
- 2 cups heavy cream
- 1 garlic clove, minced
- 1 tbsp butter
- 1 cup Gruyère cheese, grated
- Salt and pepper to taste
- Fresh thyme for garnish

Instructions:

1. Preheat the oven to 375°F (190°C). Butter a 9x13-inch baking dish.
2. In a saucepan, heat the cream with garlic, salt, and pepper over medium heat. Bring to a simmer and remove from heat.
3. Layer the potato slices in the baking dish, pouring the warm cream mixture over each layer.
4. Top with grated Gruyère cheese and cover with foil.
5. Bake for 45 minutes, then remove the foil and bake for an additional 15 minutes, until golden and bubbling.
6. Garnish with fresh thyme and serve.

Cassoulet

Ingredients:

- 1 lb dried white beans (such as Great Northern or Cannellini)
- 4 slices bacon, chopped
- 1 lb pork shoulder, cut into chunks
- 1 duck leg confit (or chicken thighs)
- 1 onion, chopped
- 2 cloves garlic, minced
- 2 carrots, peeled and chopped
- 1 can (14 oz) crushed tomatoes
- 4 cups chicken broth
- 1 tsp thyme
- 1 bay leaf
- Salt and pepper to taste
- 1/2 cup breadcrumbs (optional)

Instructions:

1. Soak the beans overnight in water. Drain and set aside.
2. In a large pot, cook the bacon until crisp, then remove and set aside. Brown the pork shoulder and duck confit in the bacon fat.
3. Add the onion, garlic, and carrots to the pot and sauté for 5 minutes.
4. Add the tomatoes, chicken broth, thyme, bay leaf, and beans. Bring to a simmer and cook for 2-3 hours, until the beans are tender.
5. Season with salt and pepper, and top with breadcrumbs if desired. Serve hot.

Chateaubriand with Béarnaise Sauce

Ingredients for the Chateaubriand:

- 2 lb beef tenderloin (center-cut)
- 2 tbsp olive oil
- Salt and pepper to taste

For the Béarnaise Sauce:

- 1/4 cup white wine vinegar
- 1/4 cup dry white wine
- 1 shallot, finely chopped
- 3 tbsp fresh tarragon, chopped
- 4 large egg yolks
- 1 cup unsalted butter, melted
- Salt and pepper to taste

Instructions:

1. Preheat the oven to 400°F (200°C). Heat olive oil in a large ovenproof skillet over high heat. Season the beef tenderloin with salt and pepper and sear on all sides until browned.
2. Transfer the skillet to the oven and roast the beef for 20-25 minutes for medium-rare, or longer for desired doneness.
3. While the beef is roasting, make the Béarnaise sauce: Combine vinegar, wine, shallot, and 1 tablespoon of tarragon in a small pan over medium heat. Reduce by half, then remove from heat and cool slightly.
4. Whisk the egg yolks into the vinegar mixture and place over a double boiler. Gradually whisk in the melted butter until thickened.
5. Remove from heat, stir in the remaining tarragon, and season with salt and pepper.
6. Slice the beef and serve with the Béarnaise sauce.

Potatoes Dauphine

Ingredients:

- 2 lbs potatoes, peeled and diced
- 1/2 cup butter
- 1/2 cup milk
- 1 cup all-purpose flour
- 4 large eggs
- 1/4 tsp nutmeg
- Salt and pepper to taste
- Vegetable oil for frying

Instructions:

1. Boil the potatoes in salted water until tender, about 10-15 minutes. Drain and mash them.
2. In a saucepan, heat butter and milk together until melted. Stir in flour to make a smooth paste (roux). Cook for 2-3 minutes over medium heat.
3. Gradually add the mashed potatoes to the roux and mix until smooth. Remove from heat and let it cool for a few minutes.
4. Beat in the eggs, one at a time, until fully incorporated. Season with nutmeg, salt, and pepper.
5. Heat oil in a deep fryer or large pot to 350°F (175°C). Use a spoon or piping bag to shape the potato mixture into small balls.
6. Fry the potato balls in batches until golden brown and crispy, about 4-5 minutes.
7. Drain on paper towels and serve hot.

Pâté en Croûte

Ingredients:

- 1 lb ground pork
- 1/2 lb ground veal
- 1/4 lb ground beef
- 1/2 lb pork fatback, chopped
- 1/2 cup Cognac
- 1/2 cup chicken stock
- 1/4 tsp ground nutmeg
- 1/2 tsp dried thyme
- Salt and pepper to taste
- 1 sheet puff pastry
- 1 egg, beaten (for glazing)

Instructions:

1. Preheat the oven to 375°F (190°C).
2. In a large bowl, combine the ground meats, fatback, Cognac, stock, nutmeg, thyme, salt, and pepper. Mix until well combined.
3. Roll out the puff pastry on a lightly floured surface and line a loaf pan with it, leaving some overhang.
4. Fill the pastry-lined pan with the meat mixture, pressing it down gently.
5. Fold the pastry over the top of the meat mixture, sealing the edges and trimming any excess.
6. Brush the top of the pastry with the beaten egg.
7. Bake for 1 hour, or until the pastry is golden and the filling is cooked through. Let cool before slicing.

Filet Mignon au Poivre

Ingredients:

- 4 filet mignon steaks (6 oz each)
- 2 tbsp black peppercorns, crushed
- 2 tbsp olive oil
- 2 tbsp butter
- 1/2 cup brandy
- 1 cup heavy cream
- Salt to taste

Instructions:

1. Coat the filet mignon steaks with the crushed black peppercorns, pressing gently to adhere.
2. Heat olive oil in a large skillet over medium-high heat. Add the steaks and cook for 3-4 minutes on each side for medium-rare, or longer for desired doneness. Remove the steaks and set aside.
3. In the same skillet, melt the butter over medium heat. Add the brandy, scraping up any browned bits from the pan. Cook for 1-2 minutes.
4. Stir in the cream and cook for another 3-4 minutes, until the sauce has thickened.
5. Season with salt and pour the sauce over the steaks. Serve immediately.

Chicken Fricassée

Ingredients:

- 4 chicken thighs, bone-in and skin-on
- 1 onion, chopped
- 2 carrots, peeled and sliced
- 2 cloves garlic, minced
- 2 tbsp olive oil
- 1/2 cup white wine
- 2 cups chicken broth
- 1/2 cup heavy cream
- 2 tbsp flour
- Salt and pepper to taste
- Fresh parsley, chopped

Instructions:

1. Heat olive oil in a large pot over medium heat. Brown the chicken thighs on both sides, about 5 minutes per side. Remove and set aside.
2. In the same pot, add the onion, carrots, and garlic. Cook for 5 minutes until softened.
3. Stir in the flour and cook for 2 minutes to make a roux. Gradually add the white wine, then the chicken broth, stirring constantly.
4. Return the chicken to the pot, cover, and simmer for 40 minutes, until the chicken is cooked through.
5. Remove the chicken and whisk the heavy cream into the sauce. Simmer for 5 minutes, then return the chicken to the pot.
6. Season with salt and pepper and garnish with chopped parsley. Serve hot.

Sole Meunière

Ingredients:

- 4 sole fillets
- 1/4 cup flour
- 4 tbsp unsalted butter
- 2 tbsp fresh lemon juice
- 1/4 cup fresh parsley, chopped
- Salt and pepper to taste

Instructions:

1. Season the sole fillets with salt and pepper, then dredge in flour, shaking off any excess.
2. In a large skillet, melt 2 tablespoons of butter over medium heat. Add the sole fillets and cook for 2-3 minutes per side, until golden and cooked through. Remove and set aside.
3. In the same skillet, melt the remaining butter. Add the lemon juice and cook for 1 minute, scraping up any bits from the pan.
4. Pour the sauce over the sole fillets and garnish with chopped parsley. Serve immediately.

Moules Marinières (Mussels in White Wine)

Ingredients:

- 2 lbs mussels, cleaned and debearded
- 2 tbsp olive oil
- 1 onion, finely chopped
- 3 cloves garlic, minced
- 1 cup dry white wine
- 1 cup heavy cream
- 1/4 cup fresh parsley, chopped
- Salt and pepper to taste

Instructions:

1. Heat olive oil in a large pot over medium heat. Add the onion and garlic and sauté for 3 minutes until softened.
2. Add the wine and bring to a simmer. Add the mussels, cover, and cook for 5-7 minutes, shaking the pot occasionally, until the mussels have opened.
3. Remove the mussels and set aside. Stir the cream into the cooking liquid and simmer for 2-3 minutes until slightly thickened.
4. Season with salt and pepper, then return the mussels to the pot. Stir in the parsley.
5. Serve hot, with crusty bread on the side.

Foie Gras au Torchon

Ingredients:

- 1 lb foie gras, cleaned and deveined
- 2 tbsp Cognac or Armagnac
- 1 tbsp salt
- 1/2 tsp black pepper
- 1/2 tsp white sugar
- Cheesecloth for wrapping

Instructions:

1. Season the foie gras with salt, pepper, and sugar. Drizzle with the Cognac and let marinate for 1 hour.
2. Lay out a large piece of cheesecloth. Place the foie gras in the center and roll it up tightly, tying the ends with kitchen twine.
3. Bring a large pot of water to a simmer over low heat. Add the foie gras and cook for 20-25 minutes, turning occasionally.
4. Remove the foie gras from the water and let it cool. Chill in the refrigerator for at least 6 hours before serving.
5. Slice and serve with toasted bread or crackers.

Gâteau de Crêpes

Ingredients for the Crêpes:

- 1 cup all-purpose flour
- 1 1/2 cups milk
- 2 eggs
- 2 tbsp melted butter
- 1/4 tsp salt

For the Filling:

- 2 cups pastry cream (or whipped cream)
- 1 tbsp powdered sugar (optional)

Instructions:

1. Make the crêpes: In a bowl, whisk together flour, milk, eggs, melted butter, and salt until smooth. Let the batter rest for 30 minutes.
2. Heat a non-stick skillet over medium heat and lightly grease it. Pour a small amount of batter into the pan and swirl to coat the bottom. Cook for 1-2 minutes, then flip and cook for another 30 seconds.
3. Remove the crêpe and set aside. Repeat with the remaining batter.
4. To assemble the gâteau: Place one crêpe on a serving plate, spread a layer of pastry cream on top, and top with another crêpe. Repeat until all the crêpes and filling are used up.
5. Optionally, dust with powdered sugar and serve chilled or at room temperature.

Tarte au Citron Meringuée (Lemon Meringue Tart)

Ingredients:

- **For the crust:**
    - 1 1/4 cups all-purpose flour
    - 1/4 cup powdered sugar
    - 1/2 cup unsalted butter, cold and cubed
    - 1 large egg yolk
    - 2 tbsp ice water
- **For the lemon filling:**
    - 1 1/4 cups sugar
    - 1/4 cup cornstarch
    - 1 1/2 cups water
    - 4 large egg yolks
    - 1/2 cup fresh lemon juice
    - Zest of 2 lemons
    - 2 tbsp unsalted butter
- **For the meringue:**
    - 4 large egg whites
    - 1/2 tsp cream of tartar
    - 1/2 cup sugar

Instructions:

1. Preheat the oven to 350°F (175°C).
2. For the crust, mix the flour, powdered sugar, and cold butter in a food processor until crumbly. Add the egg yolk and ice water, and pulse until the dough comes together. Press the dough into a tart pan and refrigerate for 30 minutes.
3. Blind bake the crust by lining it with parchment paper and filling with pie weights or dried beans. Bake for 15 minutes, remove the weights, and bake for an additional 5-7 minutes until golden. Let cool.
4. For the lemon filling, whisk together the sugar, cornstarch, and water in a saucepan. Bring to a boil, whisking constantly, until thickened. Whisk in the egg yolks, lemon juice, and zest, and cook for another 2 minutes. Remove from heat and stir in the butter until smooth.
5. Pour the lemon filling into the cooled tart crust and smooth the top. Let it cool to room temperature.
6. For the meringue, beat the egg whites and cream of tartar until soft peaks form. Gradually add sugar and beat until stiff peaks form.

7. Spread the meringue over the lemon filling, making peaks with the back of a spoon.
8. Bake the tart at 350°F (175°C) for 8-10 minutes until the meringue is golden. Let cool before serving.

Soufflé au Fromage (Cheese Soufflé)

Ingredients:

- 1 1/2 cups milk
- 4 tbsp unsalted butter
- 1/4 cup all-purpose flour
- 1 1/2 cups grated Gruyère cheese
- 4 large eggs, separated
- 1/2 tsp salt
- 1/4 tsp freshly ground black pepper
- 1/4 tsp ground nutmeg
- 1 tbsp chopped fresh chives (optional)

Instructions:

1. Preheat the oven to 375°F (190°C). Grease a soufflé dish with butter and dust with flour.
2. In a saucepan, melt the butter over medium heat. Add the flour and cook, whisking constantly, for 2 minutes to form a roux.
3. Gradually whisk in the milk, cooking and stirring until thickened, about 3-5 minutes. Remove from heat and stir in the cheese until melted and smooth.
4. Beat the egg yolks into the cheese mixture, then season with salt, pepper, and nutmeg.
5. In a clean bowl, whisk the egg whites to stiff peaks. Gently fold them into the cheese mixture, being careful not to deflate them.
6. Pour the mixture into the prepared soufflé dish and bake for 25-30 minutes, until puffed and golden. Serve immediately.

Clafoutis aux Cerises (Cherry Clafoutis)

Ingredients:

- 2 cups fresh cherries, pitted
- 1/2 cup all-purpose flour
- 1/2 cup granulated sugar
- 1/4 tsp salt
- 3 large eggs
- 1 1/2 cups whole milk
- 1 tsp vanilla extract
- Powdered sugar for dusting

Instructions:

1. Preheat the oven to 350°F (175°C). Butter a 9-inch round baking dish.
2. Arrange the pitted cherries in the bottom of the dish.
3. In a bowl, whisk together the flour, sugar, and salt. Add the eggs, milk, and vanilla, and whisk until smooth.
4. Pour the batter over the cherries and bake for 35-40 minutes, until golden and set in the center.
5. Let cool slightly, then dust with powdered sugar before serving.

Salade de Chèvre Chaud (Warm Goat Cheese Salad)

Ingredients:

- 4 slices baguette
- 4 oz goat cheese, sliced into rounds
- 4 tbsp honey
- 2 cups mixed greens
- 1/4 cup walnuts, toasted
- 1/4 cup balsamic vinaigrette

Instructions:

1. Preheat the oven to 350°F (175°C). Place the slices of baguette on a baking sheet and toast for 5-7 minutes, until golden.
2. Top each piece of toast with a slice of goat cheese and drizzle with honey.
3. Bake the toasts in the oven for an additional 5-7 minutes, until the cheese is warm and slightly melted.
4. On a serving platter, arrange the mixed greens and top with the toasted goat cheese toasts. Sprinkle with toasted walnuts and drizzle with balsamic vinaigrette.

Bouchées à la Reine (Vol-au-Vents)

Ingredients:

- 1 package puff pastry (store-bought or homemade)
- 1/2 lb cooked chicken, diced
- 1/2 cup mushrooms, sliced
- 1/4 cup butter
- 2 tbsp all-purpose flour
- 1/2 cup chicken stock
- 1/2 cup heavy cream
- 1 tbsp fresh parsley, chopped

Instructions:

1. Preheat the oven to 400°F (200°C). Roll out the puff pastry and cut into rounds. Use a smaller round cutter to cut out the center, forming a ring. Place the rings on a baking sheet and bake for 15-20 minutes until puffed and golden. Remove from the oven.
2. In a skillet, melt butter over medium heat and sauté the mushrooms for 5 minutes. Add the diced chicken and cook for another 3 minutes.
3. Stir in the flour and cook for 2 minutes, then gradually add the chicken stock and cream, stirring constantly until the mixture thickens.
4. Spoon the chicken and mushroom mixture into the puff pastry shells and garnish with chopped parsley. Serve immediately.

Croustillants de Brie (Crispy Brie Bites)

Ingredients:

- 8 oz Brie cheese, cut into small cubes
- 1 sheet puff pastry, thawed
- 1 egg, beaten
- 1/4 cup breadcrumbs
- Honey for drizzling (optional)

Instructions:

1. Preheat the oven to 375°F (190°C). Line a baking sheet with parchment paper.
2. Roll out the puff pastry and cut into squares, large enough to wrap around the Brie cubes.
3. Place a cube of Brie in the center of each square and fold the pastry around it to form a bundle.
4. Dip each bundle into the beaten egg and then coat with breadcrumbs.
5. Place the Brie bites on the prepared baking sheet and bake for 15-20 minutes, until golden and crispy.
6. Serve with a drizzle of honey, if desired.

Salade Landaise (Landes Salad)

Ingredients:

- 2 cups mixed greens
- 1/2 cup duck breast, cooked and sliced
- 1/2 cup foie gras, sliced (optional)
- 1/4 cup walnuts, toasted
- 1/4 cup crispy bacon lardons
- 1/4 cup balsamic vinaigrette

Instructions:

1. In a large bowl, combine the mixed greens, duck breast slices, foie gras (if using), toasted walnuts, and crispy bacon.
2. Drizzle with balsamic vinaigrette and toss gently to combine.
3. Serve immediately.

Poulet Basquaise (Basque Chicken)

Ingredients:

- 4 chicken thighs, bone-in, skin-on
- 2 tbsp olive oil
- 1 onion, chopped
- 1 bell pepper, sliced
- 2 tomatoes, chopped
- 1/2 cup dry white wine
- 1/4 cup chicken stock
- 2 cloves garlic, minced
- 1 tsp paprika
- Salt and pepper to taste
- Fresh parsley for garnish

Instructions:

1. Heat olive oil in a large skillet over medium-high heat. Brown the chicken thighs on both sides, about 5 minutes per side. Remove the chicken and set aside.
2. In the same skillet, sauté the onion, bell pepper, garlic, and paprika until softened, about 5 minutes.
3. Add the chopped tomatoes and cook for another 2 minutes, then pour in the white wine and chicken stock.
4. Return the chicken to the skillet, cover, and simmer for 35-40 minutes, until the chicken is cooked through.
5. Season with salt and pepper, and garnish with fresh parsley before serving.

Sauté de Veau à la Normande (Veal Stew in Normandy Style)

Ingredients:

- 2 lbs veal stew meat, cut into cubes
- 2 tbsp butter
- 1 onion, chopped
- 2 cloves garlic, minced
- 1 cup dry white wine (preferably from Normandy)
- 1 cup heavy cream
- 1/2 cup chicken stock
- 1 tbsp fresh thyme, chopped
- 1 bay leaf
- Salt and pepper to taste
- 1/2 cup fresh parsley, chopped
- 1/4 cup apple brandy (optional)

Instructions:

1. Heat the butter in a large skillet over medium-high heat. Add the veal cubes and cook until browned on all sides, about 8-10 minutes. Remove the veal and set aside.
2. In the same pan, sauté the onion and garlic until soft and golden, about 5 minutes.
3. Add the white wine to deglaze the pan, scraping up any browned bits. Let it simmer for 2-3 minutes.
4. Return the veal to the pan, add the chicken stock, thyme, and bay leaf. Bring to a boil, then reduce the heat to low and simmer for 45 minutes to 1 hour, until the veal is tender.
5. Stir in the cream and cook for another 5-10 minutes, until the sauce thickens slightly.
6. Season with salt and pepper. Stir in the fresh parsley and apple brandy (if using) before serving.

Pâtisserie Chouquettes (Choux Pastry Puffs)

Ingredients:

- 1/2 cup water
- 1/2 cup whole milk
- 1/2 cup unsalted butter
- 1 tsp sugar
- 1/4 tsp salt
- 1 cup all-purpose flour
- 4 large eggs
- Pearl sugar for topping (optional)

Instructions:

1. Preheat the oven to 375°F (190°C) and line a baking sheet with parchment paper.
2. In a saucepan, combine the water, milk, butter, sugar, and salt. Bring to a boil, stirring to melt the butter.
3. Remove from heat and add the flour all at once. Stir vigorously until the dough forms a smooth ball and pulls away from the sides of the pan.
4. Return the saucepan to the stove over medium heat and cook the dough, stirring constantly, for 2-3 minutes to dry it out slightly.
5. Remove from heat and let the dough cool for 5 minutes. Beat in the eggs, one at a time, until the dough is smooth and glossy.
6. Using a pastry bag or two spoons, drop small mounds of dough onto the prepared baking sheet.
7. Sprinkle with pearl sugar if desired, and bake for 20-25 minutes, until golden and puffed.
8. Let cool on a wire rack and serve as a snack or dessert.

Pissaladière (Provençal Onion Tart)

Ingredients:

- 1 sheet puff pastry
- 4 large onions, thinly sliced
- 2 tbsp olive oil
- 1/4 cup black olives, pitted and sliced
- 6 anchovy fillets, drained
- 1 tbsp fresh thyme leaves
- 1/4 tsp black pepper

Instructions:

1. Preheat the oven to 400°F (200°C). Line a baking sheet with parchment paper.
2. Heat the olive oil in a large pan over medium heat. Add the onions and cook, stirring occasionally, until caramelized and soft, about 25 minutes.
3. Roll out the puff pastry on the prepared baking sheet. Spread the caramelized onions evenly over the pastry, leaving a small border around the edges.
4. Arrange the olives and anchovies on top of the onions, and sprinkle with fresh thyme and black pepper.
5. Bake the pissaladière for 20-25 minutes, until the pastry is golden and puffed.
6. Let it cool slightly before slicing and serving.

Tartelette aux Framboises (Raspberry Tartlets)

Ingredients:

- 1 sheet shortcrust pastry
- 1/2 cup raspberry jam
- 2 cups fresh raspberries
- 1/2 cup heavy cream
- 1/4 cup powdered sugar
- 1 tsp vanilla extract

Instructions:

1. Preheat the oven to 350°F (175°C). Line a muffin tin with the shortcrust pastry and press into the bottoms of each cup. Prick the bottoms with a fork.
2. Bake for 12-15 minutes, until golden and crisp. Let cool completely.
3. Warm the raspberry jam in a small pan and brush a thin layer over the inside of each cooled tart shell.
4. Whip the cream with the powdered sugar and vanilla extract until soft peaks form.
5. Fill each tart shell with whipped cream and top with fresh raspberries.
6. Serve immediately or refrigerate until ready to serve.

Côtelettes d'Agneau aux Herbes (Herb-Crusted Lamb Chops)

Ingredients:

- 8 lamb chops, trimmed
- 2 tbsp olive oil
- 2 cloves garlic, minced
- 2 tbsp fresh rosemary, chopped
- 2 tbsp fresh thyme, chopped
- 1 tbsp Dijon mustard
- Salt and freshly ground black pepper

Instructions:

1. Preheat the oven to 400°F (200°C).
2. Rub the lamb chops with olive oil, minced garlic, rosemary, thyme, Dijon mustard, salt, and pepper.
3. Heat a skillet over medium-high heat. Sear the lamb chops for 2-3 minutes on each side until browned.
4. Transfer the lamb chops to the oven and roast for 6-8 minutes for medium-rare, or longer to your desired level of doneness.
5. Let the lamb rest for 5 minutes before serving.

Crêpes Suzette

Ingredients:

- 1 cup all-purpose flour
- 1 1/2 cups milk
- 2 large eggs
- 2 tbsp unsalted butter, melted
- 1/4 cup sugar
- 1/2 tsp vanilla extract
- 1/4 cup orange juice
- 1/4 cup Grand Marnier
- 1/4 cup butter
- 2 tbsp orange zest

Instructions:

1. In a mixing bowl, whisk together the flour, milk, eggs, melted butter, sugar, and vanilla extract to make a smooth batter. Let it rest for 30 minutes.
2. Heat a non-stick skillet over medium heat. Pour a small amount of batter into the pan and tilt to coat the bottom with a thin layer.
3. Cook until lightly golden on both sides, then remove and set aside. Repeat with the remaining batter.
4. For the sauce, melt butter in a skillet, then add orange juice, Grand Marnier, sugar, and orange zest. Let it simmer for a couple of minutes.
5. Fold the crêpes into quarters and place them in the sauce. Cook for 2-3 minutes, spooning sauce over the crêpes to soak them.
6. Flambé the crêpes with Grand Marnier (optional), then serve immediately.

Fennel and Orange Salad

Ingredients:

- 1 fennel bulb, thinly sliced
- 2 oranges, peeled and segmented
- 1/4 cup fresh mint, chopped
- 2 tbsp olive oil
- 1 tbsp red wine vinegar
- Salt and freshly ground black pepper

Instructions:

1. In a large bowl, combine the fennel slices, orange segments, and mint.
2. In a small bowl, whisk together the olive oil, vinegar, salt, and pepper.
3. Drizzle the dressing over the salad and toss gently to combine.
4. Serve immediately as a refreshing side dish.

Blanquette de Veau (Veal in White Sauce)

Ingredients:

- 2 lbs veal stew meat, cut into cubes
- 2 tbsp butter
- 1 onion, chopped
- 2 carrots, peeled and chopped
- 2 cloves garlic, minced
- 2 cups chicken stock
- 1 bay leaf
- 1/4 cup heavy cream
- 2 tbsp all-purpose flour
- 1 tbsp fresh parsley, chopped
- Salt and pepper to taste

Instructions:

1. In a large pot, melt butter over medium heat. Brown the veal cubes in batches and remove them from the pot.
2. In the same pot, sauté the onion, carrots, and garlic until softened, about 5 minutes.
3. Return the veal to the pot and add the chicken stock and bay leaf. Bring to a boil, then reduce the heat and simmer for 1-1.5 hours, until the veal is tender.
4. In a separate saucepan, melt butter and stir in the flour. Gradually add some of the cooking liquid to make a smooth roux.
5. Stir the roux into the veal stew, and cook for another 10 minutes. Stir in the heavy cream and parsley, and adjust seasoning with salt and pepper.
6. Serve with rice or potatoes.

Grilled Lobster with Herb Butter

Ingredients:

- 4 lobster tails, halved lengthwise
- 1/4 cup unsalted butter, melted
- 2 cloves garlic, minced
- 2 tbsp fresh parsley, chopped
- 1 tbsp fresh lemon juice
- 1 tbsp fresh thyme, chopped
- Salt and freshly ground black pepper
- Lemon wedges for serving

Instructions:

1. Preheat the grill to medium-high heat.
2. In a small bowl, combine the melted butter, garlic, parsley, lemon juice, thyme, salt, and pepper.
3. Brush the lobster meat with the herb butter mixture.
4. Place the lobster tails on the grill, shell-side down, and cook for 5-7 minutes, basting with more herb butter as they cook.
5. Turn the lobster tails over and grill for an additional 2-3 minutes, until the meat is opaque and cooked through.
6. Serve immediately with lemon wedges and additional herb butter on the side.

Chilled Vichyssoise

Ingredients:

- 3 large leeks, cleaned and sliced
- 2 medium potatoes, peeled and diced
- 4 cups vegetable stock
- 1/2 cup heavy cream
- 1 tbsp unsalted butter
- Salt and freshly ground black pepper
- Fresh chives, chopped, for garnish

Instructions:

1. In a large pot, melt the butter over medium heat. Add the leeks and sauté for 5-7 minutes, until softened.
2. Add the diced potatoes and vegetable stock to the pot. Bring to a boil, then reduce the heat and simmer for 20-25 minutes, until the potatoes are tender.
3. Remove from heat and let the soup cool slightly.
4. Use an immersion blender or regular blender to puree the soup until smooth.
5. Stir in the heavy cream and season with salt and pepper to taste.
6. Let the soup cool to room temperature, then refrigerate for at least 2 hours to chill.
7. Serve chilled, garnished with chopped chives.

Veal and Mushroom Ragout

Ingredients:

- 1 1/2 lbs veal stew meat, cut into cubes
- 2 tbsp olive oil
- 1 onion, chopped
- 2 cloves garlic, minced
- 2 cups mushrooms, sliced
- 1/2 cup white wine
- 1 cup beef or vegetable stock
- 1 tbsp fresh thyme, chopped
- 2 tbsp heavy cream
- Salt and freshly ground black pepper
- Fresh parsley, chopped, for garnish

Instructions:

1. In a large pot, heat the olive oil over medium-high heat. Brown the veal cubes in batches, then remove and set aside.
2. In the same pot, sauté the onion and garlic until softened, about 5 minutes.
3. Add the sliced mushrooms and cook until they release their moisture and start to brown, about 8 minutes.
4. Deglaze the pot with white wine, scraping up any browned bits from the bottom.
5. Return the veal to the pot and add the stock and thyme. Bring to a boil, then reduce the heat and simmer for 1 to 1.5 hours, until the veal is tender.
6. Stir in the heavy cream, and season with salt and pepper to taste.
7. Serve hot, garnished with fresh parsley.

Confit de Canard (Duck Confit)

Ingredients:

- 4 duck legs, skin-on
- 4 cups duck fat (or enough to cover the duck legs)
- 4 cloves garlic, smashed
- 2 sprigs fresh thyme
- 2 sprigs fresh rosemary
- 1 tsp black peppercorns
- 1/2 tsp salt

Instructions:

1. Preheat your oven to 250°F (120°C).
2. In a heavy, oven-safe pot (such as a Dutch oven), combine the duck legs, garlic, thyme, rosemary, peppercorns, and salt. Cover with duck fat, ensuring the legs are fully submerged.
3. Place the pot in the oven and cook for 2.5 to 3 hours, until the duck is tender and the meat pulls away easily from the bone.
4. Once cooked, remove the duck legs from the fat and set aside. You can reserve the fat for future use.
5. To crisp the skin, heat a skillet over medium-high heat and sear the duck legs, skin-side down, for 5-7 minutes until golden and crispy.
6. Serve hot, ideally with roasted potatoes or a green salad.

Sablé Bretons (Breton Shortbread Cookies)

Ingredients:

- 1 cup unsalted butter, softened
- 1/2 cup granulated sugar
- 2 large egg yolks
- 1/2 tsp vanilla extract
- 1 1/2 cups all-purpose flour
- 1/2 tsp baking powder
- Pinch of salt
- 1 egg, beaten (for egg wash)

Instructions:

1. Preheat the oven to 350°F (175°C). Line a baking sheet with parchment paper.
2. In a large bowl, beat together the butter and sugar until light and fluffy, about 3-4 minutes.
3. Add the egg yolks and vanilla extract, and continue to beat until incorporated.
4. In a separate bowl, sift together the flour, baking powder, and salt. Gradually add the dry ingredients to the butter mixture, mixing until a dough forms.
5. Roll out the dough on a floured surface to about 1/4 inch thick. Use a cookie cutter or a round glass to cut out circles of dough.
6. Place the cookies on the prepared baking sheet. Brush each cookie with the beaten egg to give them a golden finish.
7. Bake for 12-15 minutes, until the edges are lightly golden.
8. Let the cookies cool on a wire rack before serving.

Fricassée de Poulet (Chicken Fricassée)

Ingredients:

- 4 bone-in chicken thighs, skin-on
- 2 tbsp olive oil
- 1 onion, chopped
- 2 carrots, sliced
- 2 cloves garlic, minced
- 1 cup white wine
- 2 cups chicken stock
- 1/2 cup heavy cream
- 1 tbsp fresh thyme, chopped
- Salt and freshly ground black pepper
- Fresh parsley, chopped, for garnish

Instructions:

1. Heat olive oil in a large pot over medium-high heat. Brown the chicken thighs on both sides and set aside.
2. In the same pot, sauté the onion, carrots, and garlic until softened, about 5 minutes.
3. Add the white wine to deglaze the pot, scraping up any browned bits from the bottom.
4. Return the chicken to the pot and add the chicken stock and thyme. Bring to a boil, then reduce the heat and simmer for 40-45 minutes, until the chicken is cooked through.
5. Stir in the heavy cream, season with salt and pepper to taste, and cook for an additional 5 minutes.
6. Serve hot, garnished with fresh parsley.

Galette des Rois (King Cake)

Ingredients:

- 2 sheets puff pastry
- 1/2 cup almond meal
- 1/2 cup powdered sugar
- 1/4 cup unsalted butter, softened
- 1 egg
- 1 tsp vanilla extract
- 1 tbsp dark rum (optional)
- 1 egg yolk (for glazing)
- 1 fève (a small ceramic figurine or bean, traditionally hidden inside)

Instructions:

1. Preheat the oven to 375°F (190°C). Line a baking sheet with parchment paper.
2. In a bowl, mix the almond meal, powdered sugar, butter, egg, vanilla, and rum until smooth to form the frangipane filling.
3. Place one sheet of puff pastry on the prepared baking sheet. Spread the frangipane evenly on top, leaving a 1-inch border.
4. Place the fève somewhere in the filling.
5. Place the second sheet of puff pastry on top and press around the edges to seal.
6. Brush the top of the cake with egg yolk to create a glossy finish.
7. Bake for 25-30 minutes, until golden and puffed.
8. Let cool slightly before serving.

Poulet en Papillote (Chicken in Parchment)

Ingredients:

- 4 boneless, skinless chicken breasts
- 1 lemon, sliced
- 4 sprigs fresh thyme
- 1/2 cup white wine
- 1 tbsp olive oil
- Salt and freshly ground black pepper
- 4 large parchment paper sheets

Instructions:

1. Preheat the oven to 375°F (190°C).
2. Place each chicken breast on a parchment sheet. Season with salt and pepper, drizzle with olive oil, and top with lemon slices and thyme.
3. Pour a little white wine over each chicken breast.
4. Fold the parchment over the chicken to form a sealed packet. Place on a baking sheet.
5. Bake for 25-30 minutes, until the chicken is cooked through.
6. Serve immediately, opening the parchment at the table for a dramatic presentation.

French Macarons

Ingredients:

- 1 cup powdered sugar
- 1/2 cup almond flour
- 2 large egg whites
- 1/4 cup granulated sugar
- 1 tsp vanilla extract
- Food coloring (optional)

Instructions:

1. Preheat the oven to 325°F (163°C). Line two baking sheets with parchment paper.
2. Sift the powdered sugar and almond flour together into a bowl.
3. In a separate bowl, whisk the egg whites until soft peaks form. Gradually add the granulated sugar and continue to beat until stiff peaks form.
4. Gently fold the almond flour mixture into the egg whites until fully combined. Add food coloring if desired.
5. Transfer the batter to a piping bag and pipe small circles onto the prepared baking sheets.
6. Let the macarons sit at room temperature for 30 minutes to form a shell.
7. Bake for 12-15 minutes, then allow to cool completely before filling with your choice of filling (buttercream, ganache, etc.).

Pâté de Campagne (Country Pâté)

Ingredients:

- 1 lb pork shoulder, coarsely ground
- 1/2 lb pork liver, coarsely ground
- 1/4 lb pork fat, diced
- 1 small onion, finely chopped
- 2 cloves garlic, minced
- 1/4 cup cognac or brandy
- 1/4 cup heavy cream
- 1 tsp fresh thyme, chopped
- 1/2 tsp allspice
- 1/2 tsp salt
- 1/4 tsp freshly ground black pepper
- 1 sheet of puff pastry (optional, for wrapping)

Instructions:

1. Preheat the oven to 325°F (163°C).
2. In a bowl, combine the pork shoulder, liver, fat, onion, garlic, and thyme. Add the cognac, cream, allspice, salt, and pepper, and mix well.
3. Transfer the mixture to a loaf pan or terrine. Cover with parchment paper and foil, and bake in a water bath for 1.5-2 hours until firm.
4. Let the pâté cool, then refrigerate for at least 4 hours or overnight.
5. Serve with baguette slices or crackers. You can also wrap it in puff pastry and bake for a golden crust.

www.ingramcontent.com/pod-product-compliance
Lightning Source LLC
LaVergne TN
LVHW081329060526
838201LV00055B/2536